Cunt

Motherfucker

Assclown

Dumbass

Fuck
You

Breathe

Asshat

Asshole

Bitchtits

Cock

Cumwipe

Dick

Slut

Idiot

Nutsack

Shit

Thundercunt

Twat

Twatface

Dickhead

Damn

Hell

Piss

Son of a bitch

CPSIA information can be obtained
at www.ICGtesting.com
Printed in the USA
BVHW02s1323020218
506835BV00011B/158/P

9 781945 260056